CAR POEMS

poems by

Maureen McElroy

Finishing Line Press
Georgetown, Kentucky

CAR POEMS

Copyright © 2020 by Maureen McElroy
ISBN 978-1-64662-163-7 First Edition
All rights reserved under International and Pan-American Copyright Conventions. No part of this book may be reproduced in any manner whatsoever without written permission from the publisher, except in the case of brief quotations embodied in critical articles and reviews.

ACKNOWLEDGMENTS

The author would like to thank the editors of the following literary journals where versions of these poems first appeared:

Trampset "Car Poems"
Io Literary Journal "Caterpillar"

Publisher: Leah Maines
Editor: Christen Kincaid
Cover Art: William McElroy
Author Photo: Renee Dekona
Cover Design: Elizabeth Maines McCleavy

Printed in the USA on acid-free paper.
Order online: www.finishinglinepress.com
　　　　　also available on amazon.com

Author inquiries and mail orders:
Finishing Line Press
P. O. Box 1626
Georgetown, Kentucky 40324
U. S. A.

Table of Contents

Car Poems 1

Sundays at Bickford's 2

Moonlight 3

The Algarve 4

Beef Bourguignon 5

Weight 6

Early October 7

Burned 8

Mighty Woman 9

Perennial 10

Tomboy 11

My Trip to California 12

Ruth 13

Woody Station Wagon 14

The Subject of My Father's Photographs 15

Dignity 17

For Mom 18

Skinny Lady Singing 20

Lullabye Bye Baby 21

Someone I Used to Shop With 22

Stalker 24

August Heat 25

Cheap Motel in California 26

Caterpillar 27

We're Not in Oz Anymore 28

for William

Car Poems

Some people have sex in cars
like Cadillacs or little red Corvettes
with the seats rolled back
and write songs about it,
but I write poems in cars.

M-m-m-my Corolla poems,
my MINI Cooper poems,
my KIA Soul poems,
getting pulled over
for writing while driving poems.

Rear view rhymes,
stuck-in-traffic last gasp
angry poems.
Cup holders and couplets,
speed bumps and alliteration.
Rolling, rolling,
windows down,
and the city cacophony
inspiring me, driving me.

Stop signs and stanza breaks.
I take the roads less traveled
and the dark alleys,
the cut-throughs.

I write in windshield condensation,
reach under the seats to find a pen,
a napkin, a bank slip, a receipt
to get my words down
that travel with me
to my next destination.

Sundays at Bickford's

I remember Sundays at Bickford's
when we were first dating.
We smelled of each other's skin,
and our lips were raw.
My 580 square foot condo
was just enough space.

The waitress called you "honey"
in a voice that rasped with 3 packs a day.
You ate a dumpling the size of my head,
but you stayed thin and muscular,
because you woke at dawn
to work construction in Beacon Hill.

That was the happiest time in my life,
before it closed, and now the walls
of our 3-bedroom start to close in on me,
and the rasp in my voice is from shouting.

Still, I find myself on any given Sunday
making Belgian waffles and French toast,
bacon and pancakes all day,
wanting nothing more than maple syrup
and you.

Moonlight

Is it dark yet?
We glow then.
You capture me in a glass jar,
and I shine for only you.

Firelight, floating candles burn
in the river of our devotion.
We can move our hands
then from shielding our eyes.
We can move our clothes
then from shielding skin.

We can put shame to shame
in the quiet, when children
are sleeping, when hair comes down
and the harsh day is undone.

The Algarve

I fell asleep reading poetry
on a balcony in Portugal
and dreamt I was cheating
on my husband with my husband.
He wore a white linen shirt
and tasted of Duoro wine.

The houses were whitewashed
with red clay roofs.
My son jumped in the waves
of Fresia Beach, his arms akimbo,
a water bird riding his joy.

I walked away from an old woman
with a strangled voice,
as if she had been choked all her life.

At night the cats took over
with little bells jingling
on their collars.

Beef Bourguignon

I think of you at the market
as I rub sprigs of rosemary
between my fingers,
pick out new potatoes
and fresh parsley, an apple galette.
I hunger.

At home I listen to Piaf,
wash button mushrooms
grown in the bleak dark, quartered;
pearl onions peeled and softened;
chuck tender cubed and browned
in olive oil.

It takes thyme, bay leaves, garlic.
I marry the beef to wine,
a young, full-bodied burgundy,
sauteed, stewed, simmering for hours
as the beeswax candles burn down
and I finish the bottle.

My eyes are reduced to water and salt
as I watch you feed the beef bourguignon
to our bichon frise,
the sauce staining his white
corkscrew curls.

Weight

After seeing the number on the scale
I swore off pasta and wine
and all things white.
I walked eight miles and wore down
the treads of the stairs.

I closed my eyes and envisioned myself
as a leaf tossed about by the wind,
as dry and crunchy underfoot
as a potato chip.
I swore off salt and bubbles.

Oxygen was all I would take in,
oxygen and music,
and I started spinning
until I became too weak to dance.

Then I went out and bought
a larger pair of pants.

Early October

You won't turn on the heat.
Every fan is blowing.
The air conditioners
block the windows.
You walk about barefoot
in shorts and t-shirts
as I start to curl into myself,
my hedgehog pose of cold.

I add layer after layer,
the weight of wool pulling me
down as I slowly sink under
duvets, under afghans,
under an avalanche

where you will find me in November
rubbing my little sticks
of resentment together.

Burned

I was the finest bottle of wine
you had ever tasted,
but you guzzled me.
You called me Purple,
but I was Aubergine.

I was a nightingale,
a raven-haired torch singer
in a smoky room,
and like a cigarette,
you crushed me.

I was tall and strong,
a Sequoia tree.
I was a mighty tower of truth.
You were reckless, explosive.
You toppled me.

I was a rolling sea.
I was the hope, the rope,
the hand when you were drowning.
I was the cure, the Holy Grail,
and you poisoned me.

I was a masterpiece,
the eyes in the painting
that followed you.
I was your guilt, your reckoning,
so you slashed me.

I was your four-leaf clover,
your Were-Rabbit foot,
your albatross, your matrix.
I was rare. I was precious,
and you burned me,

but you forgot I was a Phoenix.

Mighty Woman

She could turn heads.
She could turn a phrase.
She was the buck stopper.
She was the static, the magnet,
the electricity in every room.

She could climb a mountain
in stilettos
and stomp out ignorance.
She could cleave granite
with her wit.

She spoke. She elevated.
She enunciated. She illuminated.
She took in slivers.
She gave in loaves.
She was *shook gold*.

She was greater than the sum
of her beautiful parts—
her arms, her lips, her hips.
She was immeasurable.
She walked on history
and brought tomorrows.

She brought it, all of it,
every day. She supplied.
She multiplied. She diffused.
She was her own muse.

She was the healer.
She was the dealer of justice.
She was lover. She was tender.
She was nectar. She was elixir.

She was half of the Universe.
She was whole.

She was mighty woman.

Perennial

I have spent so many years
with the analogy of myself
as a rose—small bud, late bloomer,
bitten between the teeth
of a Flamenco dancer,
fading, petals dropping, bloom gone,
but I have been so wrong.

I am no rose, but a rose bush,
pruned back, wintering
with resplendent thorns
and with the ability
to begin again and again.

Tomboy

I was a tomboy, the summer I was ten.
My Dad took me to a barbershop
and made them chop off all my curls,
so the old ladies at Church called me *he*.

I bounced rubber balls for hours
against the brick wall of the Cunningham School.
I wore long pants in the heat and ran faster
than all the boys who never caught me.

My lips were chapped,
my dimples full of dirt.
I read Stephen King and lay down
beneath headstones at the cemetery.
I kept a locked diary and started writing poetry.

I talked fast. I was a wiseass. I swung sticks.
My fists were up. My nails were chewed down.
I wore a blue felt fedora with a feather
I pinched off a dead bird.

I collected rocks like feldspar
and pyrite, fool's gold,
and drank from a garden hose,
and became a pitcher, and rode
my bike with no helmet full speed
down Sunnyside Street
and through the woods around the MDC Pool
where the previous summer
a stranger had molested me,
but I'm sure it had nothing to do with that.

I fell in love with boys
the summer after that.

My Trip to California

Do you remember that time
in Haight-Ashbury
where we met on the corner,
turned into amoebas,
altered our shapes,
ate cookies and Pad Thai?
My hair was waist length
and curly; your beard luxurious.
We wore sunglasses and little else.

I was a painted lady,
peace sign on my belly.
My hips were glorious.
Janis sang with Jimi,
and I read my poetry
to the anarchists,
and they snapped for me.
Even the dogs were tie dyed
and smelled of patchouli.

Everyone had the munchies,
but no one went hungry.
We lay down on blankets.
No one owned us or the land.
Love was legal.
Joy was legal.
It was the Summer of Love
and life was anointing me
with tranquility and Chai tea.

Do you remember that time?

Neither do I.

Ruth

You the boat rocker,
everyone crashing in your waves.
You the testifier,
your measured voice filling the stage.
You the naysayer, the righter of wrongs,
the gavel slammer, the black robed
mama jama. You the lace-collared
little woman standing tall,
the operatic justice maker
of biblical proportions.

Keep doing push-ups
and pushing up that ceiling,
that *foot from off our necks,*
asking no favors for our sex
and making no excuses for those
who would choke our liberty.

Speak, speak for the shadow dwellers,
for the back alley victims,
the Norma Rae's, the skirted
high-heeled or low-heeled challengers
of place, of the ladder, of the uterus,
of the vagina, against the grabbers,
against the shamers, against the unjust
justices in your ranks.

Woody Station Wagon

My Father's pride and joy in the 70s
was a woody station wagon.
He paneled the living room
and dining room to match.

We kids piled in the back,
sticky from soda and melted
red lollipops.

It smelled of chlorine
and salty Carson Beach.
Windows rolled down,
our hair drying in the wind,
and Boston exhaust seeping in.

No A.C., no seat belts—
just drive-ins and road trips,
suitcases and mattresses on the roof rack.
There were fewer cars on the road then
and no cell phones.

We were all arms and legs
with bandaids and sunburns
and stuffed animals,
squabbling and laughing and sliding
around through our childhood.

The Subject of My Father's Photographs

Over our weekly Sunday dinner
at the Village Manor,
after chicken Thai soup
and wrapped scallops,
my father's eyes tear up,
and I hand him all my napkins.
He says this happens every time he eats;
his eyes and nose run from the heat,
the spices. At 97, he has little control
over the functions of his body.

My father is a photographer.
I tell him about an exhibit I saw
at the Museum of Fine Arts in Boston,
Photographs of Families.
I tell him I've had poems accepted,
and he asks me again
"can I not write a novel?"
I love to condense a story into a small space,
a snap shot. Poetry is my medium.

I tell him of this idea I had
that I thought would be a tribute to him,
or perhaps a collaboration,
a book of his photographs along with
poems I would write about them,
a juxtaposition of our art.

I mention some of his memorable shots:
the beautiful woman in the doorway,
Mrs. Mason reading at the Copley Library,
smoke billowing from an approaching train,
children swinging from the monkey bars,

a pattern of hearts made by tire tracks
in the snow, my siblings and I
at Larz Anderson Park or tumbling
in a field of flowers, Hummels trumpeting
in front of a broken glass window.

I say there must be a story behind each image,
and he speaks to me of light and composition,
color separations, plates and paper,
his Hasellblad camera, chemicals,
and his dark room.

Then he says he's ready to be driven home,
and I realize we will always
have this disconnect,
positive and negative images,
a distance between us,
because I see the souls
that he has captured,
and he sees the shadows
that their bodies cast.

Dignity

At 97, after the loss of two wives,
quadruple bypass, hip replacement,
recurring prostate cancer,
my Dad does not wear adult diapers;
he wears "disposable underwear".

Yes, he has fallen,
but he gets back up again and again.
He feels that life is worth living
until the end. I believe he fears
the alternative, the inconceivable.

He wants all heroic measures,
full code, breathing pumps and wires,
intubation, intravenous life
if it could keep him in this world
for however long he lingers,

even if he can vaguely listen
to Judy Garland singing his favorite song—
"Somewhere Over the Rainbow."

For Mom
> *(who died of Alzheimer's Disease in 2010)*

I miss you and your Irish lullaby
and your hands that look just like mine.
I miss your laugh, and I still see you
clapping, clapping.

I didn't know you were going.
I only thought of myself,
and I grew so impatient
when you kept repeating yourself,

but tell me, tell me again
that you love me
and how you rubbed your chin
on my baby curls.

You showed love in cups of
Red Rose tea and sugar cookies,
through knitting needles.

Early mornings and late nights
your white hair would peak out
from the glass in the front door.

Your skin was so pale
and you couldn't swim
when you took us to Duxbury Beach.

I remember Arthur Fiedler
at the Boston Pops, visits to the MFA,
picnics on the Common, a thousand
baloney and potato chip sandwiches.

You gave me a typewriter
and a love of words.
You stored my drawings and poems
all those years.

You gave, and I took,
and now I want more.
Sing to me again
tora, lora, lora.
I promise to hush this time,
but I might still cry.

Skinny Lady Singing

Skinny lady's singing
and you don't know it's over.
You didn't see it coming.
You missed the 15 hours of warning.

You didn't know she knew German
or that she wore a breast plate
and a helmet with horns.

You didn't see the spear.
You didn't notice all the shattering
glass of her soprano.

The Ring Cycle is over.
The gods are no more.
Skinny lady's been singing
for a long time.
Skinny lady's getting hoarse.

Lullabye, Bye Baby

in a falling cradle
'cause the bough broke,
and Papa didn't have a rope,
but he had a bull
that could gore you,
and a bird who will mock you,
and a ring of brass.

You live in a shoe,
and the old lady whips you.
You and the dog are unfed.
You're bleeding from the head,
tumbling down a hill
or alone in a corner
terrified of spiders
and mutilated mice.

The clock is striking.
The Pied Piper is playing.
I can see how you would be
lured away.

Someone I Used to Shop With

The loss of me
looks good on you.
I saw you at the grocery.
You've picked up
a new shuffle, a limp.

You were stocking up
on frozen manly meals
and ice cream.
Don't we all need
a little artificial sweetness?

You've grown a beard
and it's gray.
You've lost some weight
under your eyes, in your wallet,
below the waist.
No more balls and chain.

No one to wake you, so you
can be sleepless all you want.
No one to care,
to stand up on her toes
to kiss you.

All those little
inconveniences of sharing
bodies and beds and meals.

You fill your trunk,
whistle to your dog Jake,
who's heading the other way.

The loss of me
looks good on you.

I saw you today.
You didn't see me.

Stalker

His love for me is so great that it is beyond words,
beyond expression, beyond the realms of this universe.
It is a silent love that resides in his eyes,
behind his sunglasses, behind cataracts.

It is a secret, sexy hush love, below a whisper
that only I can hear or feel its palpitations,
beyond the coding, beyond the pale,
so, so much love that it is trapped, really,
inside a grenade without a key,

and only I have this sixth sense of its existence,
because we are connected on another plane,
and that plane will take us away
to a tropical deserted island that is ripe for just us
(and a chef and housekeeper)
and mangoes, lots of mangoes, and a ukulele.

His love can come alive there,
and I will bask in all that light on me,
if only he would see.

August Heat

Noon has become unbearable—
hanging time, my limbs loose.
So hot, I have no more sweat.

Exhaustion overcomes me.
Blood flows slowly to my brain.
Hypothalamus is shutting down.

I'm cramping. A rash rises.
Rash decisions.
The wind reeks of festering garbage.

Tempers flare. Sirens blare.
The house fills with flies.
Wings are everywhere.

Something has died.

Cheap Motel in California

No Bible in this dive.
I think a previous guest must have
bled all over it.
This was no marital bed
in this dried up gold dust town
where ghosts wore thread-bare
blue jeans and mined for their
lost teeth, and women were so rare,
but offered themselves up
as carnations instead of orchids.

I washed myself in the bathroom,
scrubbed raw-clean with harsh soap
as you smoked before the flapjacks
and sweet syrup
and after under nature's beauty at Yosemite
where my heart expanded
and yours contracted.

I wouldn't die with you some day alone,
undiscovered for three weeks,
but I was in love in that land at 27
thinking you could be my West,
the end of my search, my final frontier.

The pan kept coming up empty.
I let go of my claim.
My skin was red from scratching.
I headed East.

Caterpillar

I've given up laughing out loud,
second chances,
hot crossed buns on Sundays,
the harpsichord.
I just sit around naked
growing body hair.

The ugly spots are spreading
down my abdomen,
but you like them there,
connect them with a ball point pen,
wrap your arms around
my squishy waist.

While you work I scribble
poems on the walls
of our jelly-glass apartment,
rub moisturizer on my splitting skin,
wait for you to bring
fresh cabbage leaves.

I used to know who I was
before you, before I—
jump up and down on the bed
poking holes with my head
through the plastic-wrapped ceiling.

I'll be hanging upside down
when you come home.
You can knock
but you can't come in
because I'm changing.

When my wings are dry
you can watch me fly
away from you.

We're Not in Oz Anymore

I am out of love.
Can I file for bankruptcy?
No court will grant
a new heart to a tin woman.

The Wizard is a fraud.
You can keep the little dog.
Your love for him is immeasurable.
I get spoonfuls
from an old recipe.

Click, click,
these high heels
don't bring me home anymore.
The monkeys, flying monkeys
throw wedding china at me.

I want to sleep in a poppy field
for a few years.

Wake me when it's over,
when the Scarecrow stops burning,
when you have found the courage
to face me,

before I melt into the floor.

Maureen McElroy was born and raised in Boston, Massachusetts as one of seven children in a close-knit Irish family. She attended Boston University and Emerson College, where she received an MFA under Joyce Peseroff and Bill Knott. Her work has appeared in numerous literary journals including *Mothers Always Write, Trampset, Io Literary Journal, Literary Hatchet,* and *Fickle Muses.* She taught English and Latin for a number of years before entering a career in real estate. She owns Jamaica Hill Realty in Boston, MA and currently lives in Milton with her husband and son.

www.ingramcontent.com/pod-product-compliance
Lightning Source LLC
LaVergne TN
LVHW041511070426
835507LV00012B/1482